J. K. Rowling: From

A Biography

J. K. Rowling was born Joanne Rowling on July 31, 1965, in Yate General Hospital in Gloucestershire, England. She was born to Peter James and Anne Volant Rowling. Her parents, who met on a train from King's Cross Station to Arbroath in 1964, were married on March 3, 1965. Her father was a soldier when her parents met; he later became an aircraft engineer for Rolls Royce. Her mother, who had been a WREN, a member of the Women's Royal Naval Service, became a science technician. When Rowling was almost two years old, her parents had her younger sister, Dianne. Two years later, they moved to Winterbourne. They lived there until Rowling was nine, at which point the family moved to Church Cottage, a home in the village of Tutshill.

Rowling began attending school when the family lived in Winterbourne. She attended St. Michael's Primary School, whose headmaster during her time, Alfred Dunn, may have been the model for Rowling's future character Albus Dumbledore. After St. Michael's, Rowling attended Wyedean School and College, where her mother was also a teacher. She was a good but not exceptional student in secondary school. However, she did become Head Girl, a student representative, and she was eager to learn. She would later base aspects of the character Hermione Granger on herself, telling an audience at the 2004 Edinburgh Book Festival, "Hermione is a bit like me when I was younger. I did not set out to make Hermione like me, but she is a bit like me. She is an exaggeration of how I was when I was younger."

It was when Rowling was a child that she began writing stories, which she would then read to her sister Dianne. Her first story, written when she was 6, was called "Rabbit." Through her great aunt Ivy, a classics teacher, she discovered Jessica Mitford, one of the famous Mitford sisters of England. The young women were the product of a minor aristocratic family. They became varying degrees of famous and infamous in the 1930s and 1940s for their exploits and political beliefs. The most infamous were Diana and Unity, who became fascists and friends with

Adolf Hitler. Unity, for her part, tried to commit suicide when World War II was declared.

Writer Jessica Mitford, on the other hand, became a communist and a civil rights activist as she grew older. It was her autobiography, *Hons and Rebels*, that Rowling's great-aunt gifted the teenager. Rowling became a great admirer of the late author and tore through all of Mitford's books.

The rest of Rowling's teenage years were not as sanguine. Her mother was diagnosed with multiple sclerosis when Rowling was 15, and her condition rapidly deteriorated. Rowling would recall seeing her mother have to crawl upstairs. At the same time, Rowling's relationship with her father was already strained. She would later say that he scared her and also told *The New Yorker*, "I did not have an easy relationship with my father." Like many teenagers throughout the 20th century, she escaped through pop music (in her case, The Clash and The Smiths) and through spending excessive time with her friends. Her best friend Sean Harris, drove a Ford Anglia, which like many of her early experiences would find its way into her book series.

For her A-Levels, which many universities in the United Kingdom use as an assessment tool to judge prospective applicants, Rowling took English, French, and German. She earned two As and one B, respectively. Seemingly ripe for success, she took the entrance exams for Oxford University in 1982 but was not admitted. Apparently, her teachers believe that admissions staff were biased against her because she attended a comprehensive school (a state school analogous to public schools in the United States). In any case, she was accepted at the University of Exeter, where she found herself studying beside students who were "frantically posh," as she told *The New Yorker*. She also told the magazine that in their presence, she reacted "not with the rage of the revolutionary but the smoldering hatred of the peasant."

Perhaps because she felt intimidated, she was not as dedicated a student in university as she was in secondary school, although she remained a voracious reader and writer. She was particularly fond of the works of Charles Dickens and JRR Tolkien, among others. However, despite her lack of interest in university, she did spend a year studying in Paris and she earned a BA in French and Classics in 1986. Her mother attended the graduation in a wheelchair.

After graduation, she put that degree to use by taking a job at the Francophone Africa desk at the London office for Amnesty International. Later, her then-boyfriend lived in Manchester, so she worked for the Chamber of Commerce, although her stay there was so abbreviated that there exists no record of it. She kept writing, though, and the University of Exeter's journal *Pegasus* published an essay she wrote called, "What was the Name of that Nymph Again? or Greek and Roman Studies Recalled." However, the inspiration for her most famous creation was just around the corner.

One day in 1990 as she was returning to London, she was struck by an idea. As she told *The Scotsman* newspaper, "All of a sudden, the idea for Harry just appeared in my mind's eye. I can't tell you why or what triggered it. But I saw the idea of Harry and the wizard school very plainly. I suddenly had this basic idea of a boy who didn't know who he was, who didn't know he was a wizard until he got his invitation to wizard school. I have never been so excited by an idea."

While Rowling was mapping out the idea for a seven-novel series, she also worked on another novel, one meant for adults. Six months after she began writing, in December 1990, Rowling's mother died after a ten-year battle with multiple sclerosis. She was 45. Although Rowling had visited her mother less than a week before, she hadn't realized the severity of her mother's condition. While her mother was frail, Rowling had been watching her weaken for so long that it didn't seem unusual.

Rowling's grief over her mother's death had profound effects. The ones that could be called positive were that she was able later to channel her grief into writing about her character Harry Potter's own feelings at the loss of his parents. More immediately were the negative effects. Not only Rowling had also just ended her long relationship with the Mancunian man, but she was also laid off from an office job she'd held. The triple losses sent her running.

Seeing an advertisement in *The Guardian* seeking English teachers in Portugal, she jumped at the chance for a fresh start. She spent her days writing, while teaching in the evening and then going out with her coworkers. Maria Ines Augiar, the assistant director of the Encounter English School, told *The Scotsman* that she remembers her friend as both "anxious" and "desperate for love." That was perhaps why, when Rowling met journalism student Jorge Arantes, she fell hard and fast.

Their relationship was tumultuous from the beginning. On one of their first dates, Arantes openly flirted with other women. Rowling responded by giving him an ultimatum—to choose between them and her. He chose her, but the incident marked the volatility and insecurity that would follow.

As their relationship developed, Rowling was the breadwinner while Arantes spent her money and claimed he was job-searching. At the time, Portugal had compulsory military service, which Arantes had not completed. Only a few months into their relationship, he was readying to complete his eight months when Rowling got pregnant. She moved in with Arantes's mother while he was away.

Sadly, Rowling miscarried. This shared tragedy served to bring her and Arantes closer together, and on August 28, 1992, he proposed. Friends in Portugal, like Augiar, who remember Arantes only in negative terms, were shocked Rowling accepted. These friends even related a disturbing event to which they were a witness, one when Arantes shoved Rowling so hard during an argument in public that strangers notified the police. The argument had taken place at a cafe across the street from Encounter, where Rowling had fled. When the police arrived, Arantes was shouting at the school, "Joanne, forgive me, I love you." It was only a little while later that Rowling was returning those shouts of love.

Rowling and Arantes were married on October 16, 1992, at the registry office in Porto. Rowling's sister Dianne and Dianne's boyfriend served as witnesses, while Peter Rowling did not attend. He had moved in with his secretary and would marry her that year, two years after Anne Rowling's death, moves that would deepen the rift between father and daughters. And while Peter Rowling is still married to his former secretary Jan, his eldest daughter's first marriage lasted only 13 months and 1 day, all of which was spent in Arantes's mother's home.

Two months after the wedding, Rowling found out that she was pregnant again. It likely wasn't long after that—and could have even been before that—that her friends started encouraging her to leave Arantes. However, Rowling stayed. July 27, 1993, she gave birth to her first child, her daughter Jessica, named for Rowling's favorite Mitford sister.

When Jessica was two months old, Arantes and Rowling had an

argument that ended in Arantes throwing his wife out of the house. As he later told *The Daily Express*, "She refused to go without Jessica, and, despite my saying she could come back for her in the morning, there was a violent struggle. I had to drag her out of the house at 5 in the morning, and I admit I slapped her very hard in the street." Rowling returned later that day with friend Augiar and a policeman and was able to retrieve Jessica. For the next two weeks, she and her daughter hid from Arantes by staying with friends he didn't know. Then Rowling took her daughter (and three chapters about a character named Harry Potter) back to the United Kingdom. Rowling's sister Dianne and her husband Roger opened their home in Scotland to Rowling and Jessica. Upon her return, she told *The New Yorker*, "I was very depressed. I felt life was a train wreck. I'd carried this baby out of it, and I was in this place that was very alien and cold, and quite grim.

Rowling and Jessica lived with Dianne and Roger for a few weeks but then moved into an apartment that was provided by social services. Eventually, she was able to move into another apartment, thanks to a loan from her friend Sean Harris. It was also through the help of friends that she managed to furnish the apartment for herself and Jessica. Although this part of Rowling's life has been mythologized in the aftermath of her success, for Rowling, it was neither as harrowing or as charming as it has been portrayed.

This is because while she wasn't so poor that she had to choose between food and typewriter ribbons, as has been portrayed, she still had struggles. One of these struggles was still Arantes, who showed up in Scotland allegedly trying to reconcile with his wife. He would later tell *The Daily Express* that while his plans for reconciliation were fruitless, "Fortunately, I found another girl for the rest of my holiday, but it upset me that when I was leaving, she would not let me see Jessica." Rowling filed for the Scottish equivalent of an order of protection and in 1994, filed for divorce.

Meanwhile, she still had to find a way to support herself. She decided to pursue teaching but also decided to defer her enrollment until she'd finished writing her book. To do so, she had to go on welfare. Finding it difficult to write without becoming distracted, Rowling finally visited a doctor, who diagnosed her with depression. Rowling ultimately credits her daughter for this, telling *The New Yorker*, "It was Jessica—I have to credit her with so much—that gave me the impetus to go and say to a doctor, 'I think I'm not quite right, and I need some help here.' Having done that made a massive difference." Rowling began therapy and got back to work on her book.

As the mythology around the writing of her books has grown, so too has even the places where she wrote. One of the most famous is the now-shuttered Nicolson's. Despite any of the stories that may have sprung up about why she wrote there, the truth is her brother-in-law owned it, and so it was easier for her to get away with a single coffee for hours. When she wasn't at Nicolson's, she wrote at Elephant House, a tea and coffee shop who now trumpets their association with Rowling, featuring her on their homepage. Although Nicolson's is now closed, the Chinese buffet that sits in its place still receives visiting Rowling fans.

Of course, it was probably hard for Rowling to see this as her future when she was writing her first book by hand, then typing a second draft on a used manual typewriter. While she never reached the Victorian-level poverty that has sometimes been ascribed to this period of her life, it is true that she had to type multiple copies of her book whenever she wanted to change anything.

This was Rowling's routine. When Jessica fell asleep, Rowling would push her daughter in her stroller to a cafe and write. Then she would return home in the evening and write some more. Finally, she finished her first book in 1995, the same year she began studying at Edinburgh University's Moray House for a post-graduate certificate of education in modern languages. She immediately began sending chapters to agents.

The first agent returned her chapters so fast that she told the Urbanette website "it seemed like they sent it back the same day it arrived." However, as she also told the site, "The second agent, however, wrote back and asked to see the rest of the manuscript. It was one of the best letters I had ever seen, and it was only two sentences long." The second agent was from Christopher Little Literary Agents, and after seeing the full manuscript, they began sending it to publishers. In a move that surely all of them would later regret, every publisher rejected *Harry Potter and the Philosopher's Stone*. That is, all of them except for Harper Collins and Bloomsbury. Bloomsbury was faster in getting back to the agency, so they won the rights to the book. Rowling received an advance that has been listed as both £1500 and £2500.

Harry Potter and the Philosopher's Stone was published in June 1997. The author's name was listed as J. K. Rowling because Rowling's agent, Barry Cunningham, believed that boys would be attracted to the book because of the male title character and would be more likely to read a book by an author they thought was male as well. As Rowling has no middle name, she chose the K for Kathleen, her paternal grandmother.

The book centers on its title character, Harry Potter, who discovers that he has magical powers when he's invited to attend Hogwarts School of Witchcraft and Wizardry. Along the way, he makes friends with some of his fellow students, like Ron Weasley and Hermione Granger, and learns about Lord Voldemort, the evil wizard who wants to rid the world of "Muggles," or non-magical folk.

The initial print run for the book was 500 copies, which was typical for first novels. *The Scotsman*, through its writer Lindsey Fraser, published what is believed to have been the first review. It was positive, and other positive reviews followed from newspapers around the United Kingdom.

Meanwhile, the book went on to win awards, including the National Book Award.

It also won the gold medal in the category for 9-to-11-year-olds in the Nestlé Smarties Book Prize. The books in these awards are shortlisted by adults and then children select the winners in a vote. This had the effect of spreading the book even further.

Scholastic bought the United States rights to the book, which would be renamed *Harry Potter and the Sorcerer's Stone* in the United States, at the Bologna Book Fair in 1997, paying $105,000. From that, Rowling was able to buy an apartment. She already began work on the second book with help from an £8000 grant from the Scottish Arts Council. Harry Potter and the Sorcerer's Stone was released in the United States in September 1998, where it garnered mostly positive reviews and made *The New York Times* Best Sellers list.

By the time the book was published in the United States, the second book, *Harry Potter and the Chamber of Secrets*, had already been released. Warner Brothers also bought the film rights for the first two books that year; they would go on to distribute the other films as well. The second book is the one in which Rowling's old friend Sean's Ford Anglia makes an appearance. In the book, it serves as the Weasley family car and the original art for the UK release depicted the car on the cover. The book focuses on Harry's second year at Hogwarts and a prophecy involving the titular Chamber of Secrets.

Like the first book, it received generally positive reviews and sold well. Rowling won the Smarties prize again for it, as she would also do for the third book, *Harry Potter and the Prisoner of Azkaban*. This made her the first author to win the Smarties prize three years in a row. After that, she would ask to be excused from consideration, because she felt it would be fairer to other authors.

Harry Potter and the Prisoner of Azkaban was released in the United Kingdom in July 1999 and in the United States in September 1999. It finds Harry in his third year at Hogwarts, where he and friends Ron and Hermione seek information on a prisoner, Sirius Black, who escaped from Azkaban; a prison for wizards. It was a best-seller like its predecessors. In fact, it sold almost 70,000 copies in its first three days of release in the United Kingdom alone. It was also critically acclaimed and garnered

Rowling literary awards, including the Whitbread Children's Book Award and the Bram Stoker Award.

It was followed by *Harry Potter and the Goblet of Fire*, the fourth book in the series. This book was the first in the series, though, to be released simultaneously in the United States and in the United Kingdom. It was released in both countries in July 2000. It would go on to another first, the first and only Harry Potter book to win the Hugo Award, an award given to the best science-fiction or fantasy books of the year. As with the previous books, young Harry is still in Hogwarts and learning more about the wizarding world. Specifically, he is mysteriously entered into the Triwizard Tournament, a contest of magic between Hogwarts and two other wizarding schools.

Although no Harry Potter book followed in 2001, the first movie was released that year. Directed by Chris Columbus, *Harry Potter and the Philosopher's Stone* was released on November 16, 2001. Rowling had considerable creative input with the film and with all the subsequent movies. For example, she had script approval, and the studios and producers followed her edict that the casts should be entirely British.

The film generally received positive reviews, but its box office performance left no ambiguity. It was the highest grossing film of the year, as well as the second highest grossing film of all time. It would hold similar records—highest opening weekend, highest 5-day Thanksgiving weekend, etc.-- for at least a year. It still has impressive box office returns, although it falls to #78 on the highest grossing movies of all time when all of them are adjusted for inflation.

That same year, in 2001, Rowling bought a house in Scotland called Killiechassie, in an area 74 miles north of Edinburgh. She also remarried, in a ceremony at the house, to Neil Murray, a doctor. They've gone on to have two children together, David Gordon Rowling Murray, born in 2003, and Mackenzie Jean Rowling Murray, born in 2005.

The following year, in 2002, the second Harry Potter film was released. It was also directed by Chris Columbus. Like the first film, it was a critical and commercial success. Though while it broke many commercial records, it had the misfortune of being released the same year as another cultural juggernaut, *Lord of the Rings: The Two Towers*, which claimed the spot of highest grossing film. *Harry Potter and the Chamber of Secrets* came in second.

The next Harry Potter book, *Harry Potter and the Order of the Phoenix*, was released the following year, in 2003. This book features the reappearance of the Dementors, the guards of Azkaban. They are a foul species who suck the joy from people and are unsurprisingly, inspired by Rowling's own struggles with depression. The book also features the Order of the Phoenix, a group founded to fight Lord Voldemort, who has secretly returned.

By the time the book was released, it had been three years since a new Harry Potter book had been published. By that point, the fandom had only grown. So, while the book earned general critical praise and won some awards, it also marked the culture that was growing around the Harry Potter world. Pre-order sales were phenomenal, and fans lined up outside bookstores to buy the book at midnight on the day of release. It sold five million copies on its first day.

It was followed the next year by the release of the next film in the series, *Harry Potter and the Prisoner of Azkaban*. In a departure, this one was directed by Alfonso Cuarón. It was the first Harry Potter filmed released in IMAX theaters and the last to be released on VHS. Like the films before it, it did well at the box office, although it came in second to *Shrek* as the year's biggest earner. However, it is the lowest grossing film in the franchise, although it is generally regarded as the best. The website Rotten Tomatoes, which aggregates reviews from film critics, gives it a rating of 91% positive reviews.

Harry Potter and the Half-Blood Prince, the sixth book in the series, was released in July 2005. This book perhaps delves the deepest into Lord Voldemort's history and the lead-up to Harry Potter's battle with the evil wizard. In the lead-up to the book's release, almost 1.5 million pre-orders were placed through Amazon alone. Nine million copies sold worldwide within 24 hours of its actual release. In addition to its commercial success, the book was also generally praised by critics.

That November, the next film in the series, *Harry Potter and the Goblet of Fire*, was released. It was directed by Mike Newell. It broke several box office records, like the films that came before it, and was the highest grossing film internationally that year. It also received generally positive reviews.

Both the next Harry Potter book and film were not released until 2007. The book was the final book in the series, *Harry Potter and the Deathly Hallows*. It sold almost eleven million copies within the first 24 hours of its release and holds the Guinness World Record for most novels sold within a day. In this book, after years of preparation, Harry Potter and friends finally face Lord Voldemort. It was received with critical praise, and it also won some awards, including being named one of *The New York Times* 100 Notable Books.

The film version of *Harry Potter and the Order of the Phoenix* was released in July 2007. It was directed by David Yates. It came in second place for highest film earnings that year after *Pirates of the Caribbean: At World's End*. In addition, its reviews were generally positive, although it was not as highly rated as its predecessor.

Yates would go on to direct the next film in the series, Harry Potter and the Half-Blood Prince, released in 2009, as well as the final films, the movie version of *Harry Potter and the Deathly Hallows*, which was split into two parts. The first part was released in 2010 and the second followed a year later. Part 2 is the highest grossing Harry Potter film.

Although Rowling has not written about Harry Potter since 2007, she has continued to build the world around him. For example, in a continued partnership with Warner Brothers, she has written films about Newt Scamander, a character who lived in the wizarding world almost a full century before the events of the Harry Potter books. She also opened the website Pottermore in 2011, where all future Harry Potter material (outside of books) will be released. In addition, Universal Parks & Resorts is home to the Wizarding World of Harry Potter, theme areas within the parks where visitors can pretend they're in Harry's world. All told, the Harry Potter brand is worth almost $15 billion.

After finishing writing the bulk of Harry's world, however, Rowling moved on to books meant for adults. Her first book in that vein was *The Casual Vacancy,* published in 2012 by the Blair Partnership, a new literary agency founded by Neil Blair, a former employee of the Christopher Little agency. Set in the fictional British town of Pagford, it chronicles the fight between citizens for a seat on the town council after a member dies. It received mixed reviews, with many critics comparing it unfavorably to the Harry Potter books. Specifically, several critics, including Michiko

Kakutani of *The New York Times*, felt it lacked the world-building of the Potter series. Nevertheless, it was made into a miniseries for British television in 2015.

In 2013, the publisher Little Brown released *The Cuckoo's Calling*, a detective novel about an investigator called Cormoran Strike that was purportedly by an author called Robert Galbraith. A couple of months after its April release, India Knight, a columnist with the British paper The Sunday Times tweeted that it was impressive for a first novel. In response, someone named Jude Callegari tweeted that the author was actually Rowling. (It would later be revealed that Callegari was friends with someone whose husband worked for Rowling's legal team. In a gesture of apology, the company, Russells Solicitors, donated to charity in Rowling's name and returned her legal fees.) When the news was made public, sales of the book shot up.

Rowling has continued the Cormoran Strike series, releasing *The Silkworm* in 2014 and *Career of Evil* in 2015. The fourth book in the series, *Lethal White*, was supposed to have been released in 2017, but has been delayed. Rowling has explained that book will be longer than the previous ones and subsequently, the plotting is taking some time. All three books released so far have been adapted for the television in the United Kingdom, under the title *Strike*. They will air in the United States in 2018 under the name *C.B. Strike*.

Besides her work, Rowling is well-known for her philanthropic efforts, which have been funded by the proceeds from her work. In 2000, she established the Volant Charitable Trust. It has an annual budget of £5.1 million, which it distributes to a number of different causes, including organizations that fight poverty, support single parents, and research multiple sclerosis. Regarding the latter, Rowling donated £10 million in 2006 to Edinburgh University to establish a clinic that would later be named the Anne Rowling Regenerative Neurology Clinic. In 2010, she donated the same sum again. In total, she has given away an estimated $160 million, unsurprising for a woman who once said, "I think you have a moral responsibility, when you've been given far more than you need, to do wise things with it and give intelligently."

In 2011, the Leveson Inquiry was established to investigate the conduct of the British press in the wake of the *News of the World* hacking scandal. It had been revealed through investigations by *The Guardian* and other publications that employees of the News International corporation had made a practice of hacking the phones of celebrities and other notable people in order to publish exclusives. In one of the most stomach-turning examples, journalists had hacked into the phone of missing 13-year-old British schoolgirl Milly Dowler. In doing so, they'd deleted some voicemails left for the girl, which not only erased possible evidence, but also gave her family and police renewed hope that she was still alive and had perhaps just run away. Instead, her body would be discovered six months after she went missing.

Although Rowling was never a victim of the hacking, she testified before the Leveson Inquiry in regard to other treatment she'd received from the press. She described how a journalist had posed as a tax official, for example, when meeting Rowling's husband in order to get him to divulge their address. Another journalist slipped a note for Rowling in her then-5-year-old daughter's school bag. The intrusions into her life by the press had become so overwhelming, in fact, that she testified that the family had had to move. Rowling was later incensed that then-Prime Minister David

Cameron did not fully implement the recommendations of the Inquiry.

In fact, she wrote an editorial for *The Guardian* in response, titled, "I feel duped and angry at David Cameron's reaction to Leveson." The subtitle was "If the prime minister didn't want to implement the report, why were people like me asked to relive our painful experiences in public?" The editorial is one of several she's written for publications like *The Guardian* and *Time*.

Rowling, of course, continues to write fiction, planning to write the remainder of the films in the Newt Scamander series, for example. She lives with her family somewhere in Scotland, perhaps in Edinburgh. The exact location has remained hidden, due to Rowling's past experiences with the press and other intruders.

Made in the USA
Coppell, TX
03 March 2021